Thinking at 3 AM

Selected new poems

by Gerald T. Perkoff

iUniverse, Inc.
New York   Bloomington

Thinking at 3 AM
Selected new poems by Gerald T. Perkoff

Copyright © 2010 by Gerald T. Perkoff

All rights reserved. No part of this book may be used or reproduced by any means, graphic, electronic, or mechanical, including photocopying, recording, taping or by any information storage retrieval system without the written permission of the publisher except in the case of brief quotations embodied in critical articles and reviews.

The views expressed in this work are solely those of the author and do not necessarily reflect the views of the publisher, and the publisher hereby disclaims any responsibility for them.

iUniverse books may be ordered through booksellers or by contacting:

iUniverse
1663 Liberty Drive
Bloomington, IN 47403
www.iuniverse.com
1-800-Authors (1-800-288-4677)

Because of the dynamic nature of the Internet, any Web addresses or links contained in this book may have changed since publication and may no longer be valid.

ISBN: 978-1-4502-1959-4 (sc)
ISBN: 978-1-4502-1960-0 (dj)
ISBN: 978-1-4502-1958-7 (ebk)

Printed in the United States of America

iUniverse rev. date: 6/21/2010

Contents

Introduction ix
Acknowledgements xi
Part One - Inexorable Time 1
   Thinking at 3 AM 3
   Chrysalis 8
   For Quietude 9
   Death, My Constant Companion 10
   That Black Velvet Place 12
   Lady of the Night 14
   I Wish 15
   The College Admissions Essay of an Eighty-Year-Old
      Man 16
   Even at Eighty-Two 24
   Piano Class 25
   The Eighty-Year-Old Piano Student 26
   Watching the Man in the Moon After Sixty-Two Years . . 28
   The Autumn of Life 29
   A Literal Man's Thoughts on Eternity 30
   My Wants 31
   Old Age is the Cage Where the Infant Stays 33
   Will I Know It When I Am Gone? 35
Part Two - My Jewish Heart 37
   I Am a Jew 39
   An Old Jewish Man Remembers Christmas 42
   Kaddish 44

Late Erev Shabbat 46
Erev Rosh Hashonah 5769/2008. 47
My Grandson the Red Bearded Cantor 48
From Zayda, With Love 49
Part 3 – Shades 53
Night Stories 55
Sixties Flashback 59
It's the Boogie! 66
The Biplane Bicycle 68
Night Driving 70
5917a Theodosia 72
Part 4 - Those I Love 73
Marion's Visit to the Amish 75
After a Visit 77
The Well of Loneliness 78
A Promise Kept 89
Mom at Sixty-Eight. 90
The Color of Love 91
Part 5 - Looking Around Me 93
The Apple Tree 95
Voyeur. 96
6:30 am 97
Eventide 98
The Autumn Solstice. 99
Cold Autumn Tree 100
Black Hummingbird 101
Summer Morning 102
Summer Night 103

Part 6 - Meditations 105
   Locker Room 107
   The Shadow of Your Smile 108
   Sounds 109
   The Potter.................................. 110
   What Would Peace Look Like? 112
   Visiting Old Notebooks 113
   For Jim 114
   Raindrops on the Eaton Sculpture................ 116
   Lady, Are You There? 117
Part 7 - Coming of Age......................... 121
   Fatty, Fatty, Run for Your Life! 123
Notes 161

Introduction

I have always considered myself an unlikely person to write poetry. My brother, Stuart Z. Perkoff, was the poet in our family. After Stuart's untimely death from lung cancer at age forty-four, I spent eight years collecting his work and was immersed in poetry for that entire period. With the assistance of Allen Ginsberg, who wrote to the publisher on my behalf, Stuart's collected works, *Voices of the Lady*, were published in 1998 by the National Poetry Foundation at the University of Maine, Orono, ME. Even then I had no real thought of writing poetry myself.

However, I learned we have little control over these things. Poems began coming to me ten years ago, essentially out of the blue, and I now have published two books of poems before this one. The first, *Is It All Right, Stuart?* (2005), explored my family, and included random thoughts about the world around me. In my second book, *The Story of a Marriage* (2007), I told the story of my wonderful, sixty-two years long marriage to Marion.

As I have gotten older—I am eighty-three as I write this—I find myself writing about the passage of the years, about the approach of the end of my life, and about death itself. These poems make up the first section of this book. As a counterpoint, poems of autobiographical memories, poems about nature, and a long poem about my growing up also inhabit this new volume.

No writer can be certain of his readers' responses to his work. It is my hope that each reader will find something worthwhile among the many poems in this book.

Gerald T. Perkoff
Columbia, MO

Acknowledgements

I could not have completed this work without the help of Mrs. Carole Patterson, Mrs. Marcia Moskowitz, and Dr. William Bondeson. I thank them for their very helpful suggestions. Carole Patterson also took my photograph for the cover of this book. Thanks too to Mrs. Frances Raper for allowing me to photograph her lovely grandfather's clock for the book cover. I also took the photograph of the pocket watch.

I am especially grateful to Marion, who has listened to every poem and remains my most valuable critic.

To Marion

Part One - Inexorable Time

Thinking at 3 am

The house is quiet at 3 am, no creaking,
no sound except for the small bells
that always ring in my ear. It is as though
    the house and kitchen
    and floor and chair
    are there only as a cocoon
    for my thinking.

An old man's thoughts do not
    lack consistency.
As man for eons has seen himself the keeper,
    so do I
still take on the role of provider and protector,
even though my physical strength has long since
    leaked out to puddle
    on the floor.

Yes, I sit in the quiet of early morning,
    and measure in my mind
    the frailty that keeps us upright,
the razor edge between safety and danger,
the short distance between the life we live
    in the manner of the past and
the next set of rooms and floorboards which
    await us.

Of course I said "us." It has been "us"
    all our lives.
Yet I know all the basics of the things
    that make us leave.
I know human creatures describe a finite arc, I know
that one day soon, one of us will slide down
      the descending limb of that arc and
    I know that the remaining one
will be alone.

I've always been told, "don't think so much,"
    and Marion says
I shouldn't be thinking these thoughts,
    writing these words,
      but they rumble along the tracks in my mind
    without ceasing, a
locomotive whose smoke makes
    my eyes water.
Only if the drops coalesce do they call it crying.

Others have said that our time here is wasted,
    that our material goods
were collected to no avail, and surely,
    to some extent
    that is true.
They say that our time on this round ball
    that hurtles aimlessly

through space
accomplishes nothing,
and if you look only at the collective,
that too is true.
As a group, men wreak mainly destruction
and pain.

But men and women who go through the years
as pairs accomplish wonders, at least this is true
for those who know the secret and live by it.
They know that mutual respect rounds out love and
makes it work,
that the children who result from the pairing
are creatures of infinite value
who are given to us so we can
show ourselves as truly human,
that these pairs are the suns and the children
are their moons.
This is an accomplishment not just of biology
but of love,
something only individuals can manifest,
groups do not have it.

I have watched others whose partners
have gone beyond the rim of the canyon
into its depths,
and even those who never lived by the secret
have only raw, seeping edges left

where the other was attached.
They bleed, clot, bleed, look down with disbelief
    at their remaining half self,
they scar and they cripple.

What would I do if she went over the edge?
What would she do if I did?

I look around the house for a file cabinet
    that stores the
    secrets of life,
but even in a quiet house
at 3:50 AM--time does not wait even for
ruminations--there is no file,
no formula for the next step, no way
even to know how close the trail is to the
    edge of darkness.

The train in my mind never shuts down, but
even its engine needs water, coal, and oil
for the parts that rub together, so
there are stations for rest and repair, and
I have pulled into one just in time.

To Be Continued

7:00 AM

It is morning.
My locomotive is watered and coaled, and it
chugs out of the station, down the track.
 Even in daylight, the fog lies heavy
  over the path.

I cannot slow the engine. We race
down the track together,
my mind, Marion, and me,
expecting that at some railroad crossing,
at some out of the way country place,
perhaps in the daytime, perhaps at night,
someone will stall on the track as we
 hurtle forward,
and we will crash.

Chrysalis

The old emerge slowly from sleep, like
butterflies from their chrysalis,
wings tentative, steps uncertain,
not quite ready to fly.

Does the butterfly ache, as I do,
as he moves from darkness to light?

Does he too begin his day
in an envelope of silence,
taking in the small sounds
that come from nearby hills
and restless waters?

And when he escapes
the earth and flies, does he
remember his earlier fragility?

Or does he do as the old
dream of doing,
fling caution to the winds
and ride the updrafts of his
all too brief time?

For Quietude

I avoid
acrimony. It detracts from the quiet
my soul needs
to cross the infinite space between
where I am and where I want to be.

It clogs my path with the soot
of long-shed tears, and burns my feet
like fiery coals must burn ecstatics
who walk them oblivious
to reality.

Time runs from me like foaming surf
that sinks into the sand.

How fragile are the ties
that bind us to life;
how foolish to wet them
with the acid of anger.

Death, My Constant Companion[1]

We first met in 1955,
and he has followed me discreetly ever since,
his dark robe and hood showing faceless patience,
his long scythe loaded but not yet cocked.
He has waited far more years than I
    ever expected,
someone I know but do not fear, accept
    but do not love.

No, my only fear is of the path
    the scythe will
    one day take.
Will it be sudden? Painful? Prolonged?
Will it gouge my mind so I dwindle
    through long years
    of dementia?

But even these questions pale beside
    the loss of those
    I will leave behind.
For my eternity is here,
embodied in the unrealized futures
    of my children
    and theirs,

a loss that looms as a misty figure who walks
beside my dark-robed companion.
They make a formidable couple indeed.

I pray they will remain patient with me.

That Black Velvet Place[2]

Unconscious but strangely aware,
I found myself in a black velvet space,
tinged reddish and curving slightly to the left.
I must have floated there, for nothing
touched me, yet I was there long enough to be sure
    I had never been
      there before.

I had no fear,
and no understanding as we know it in
    conscious terms.
It was a peaceful place, and it had
a softness I could feel without touching.

I do not know how long I was there.
I controlled nothing,
could not go forward or back of
    my own volition,
yet I did come back,
for the black disappeared,
and I woke in the world I knew.
But I also knew I had been somewhere special,
that had I stayed I would have known
    I had died.

I had no fear then, nor do I now,
but I awoke with the certain knowledge that
    only love is important, that
      family is love,
        friendship is love,
          sunshine and rain and
            trees are love.
The rest is trivia, enjoyable perhaps,
but unimportant.

I wish I knew what most want to know,
is there a place on the other side,
at the end of the velvet black?

I cannot say,
but others say they have been there, to a place
of brilliance and light,
of beauty and peace and sights beyond imagining,
and though I doubted them at first,
I now think this.
Had I taken hold of the velvet and made
    myself stay,
I would be sitting in God's lap today.

Lady of the Night

A lady of the night
floats toward me,
her arms and hands and sensuous hips
outlined by an infinite light
that shines into my heart.

Oh, I know she is fantasy,
never to be touched.
Yet I love it that she picked me to see her,
for nothing restores like
the lights that radiate
as she turns and bends
in her private dance.

Soon she will move on
to do the same for another,
who, like me, will smile
as she raises her chin that subtle bit
that gives confidence
to true beauty.

I Wish

I have no interest in
dying before tomorrow,
and do not fear the coming days.

But I do wish
I could mark the path
for the young
in a sign language
that would penetrate
their hearts.

I would teach them
that life's work
is complete each day,
but never completed,
that time erases material things,
but love returned
is the true embodiment
of what matters.

The College Admissions Essay of an Eighty-Year-Old Man

"Why on earth should we take you?"
you say in disbelief,
only half-hiding smirks and smiles
    at the notion that
    you should permit
    an eighty-year-old man
    to join the
    young men
    in baggy pants,
and the girls with jeans so tight they seem
    painted on.

Well, I'll tell you why.

I want to bask in the light that shines behind the eyes
    of the one in ten of those
    inside whose head is
    the hot light of ambition
    and the glow of banked
    coals of learning,
ready to be blown into life.

I was like that once, storming through books
    that lay on boards
    across a tub of cold water
    I sat in to allay
    the Midwest heat.
I sat chest deep in the water, absorbing the words
    of Nobelists and
    aspirants to that prize
    who opened their brains
    for me to carefully spoon out
    my allotted share of their
    desire to solve, integrate,
    understand, and use.

I once relished weighty books that now hide
    in space in some library
    called "online,"
no card is needed,
there are no stacks with that wonderful musty smell
    of ink and paper and
    binding boards
    that signal silence,
so ideas can tip-toe off the page
    and stand
looking up at me, appealing for a small ladder
    to climb up
    to take their place
    as links in the chain

    that builds concepts
    in my head.

But I digress. You only need to know
    that I have learned
    where the keys
    to online libraries
    are hidden,
and that I can and will use these unsentimental and
    odorless storage places
    out in space.

My, you are insistent, but so you should be,
to protect the valuable spot I would take
    from some youth
    if you let me in.

"What," you ask, "would an old man like you
bring to our place of learning?" and "what," you ask,
    "would you do
    with all you took away
    in the few
    yet unnumbered years
    remaining of your stay
    in this earthly realm?"

This is a harder question to answer,
for the years stack up one by one, each compressing

      its predecessor into
      a narrow block to fit the
      space limitations of time.

But here are some of my attributes your school
      may find of use.
Surely you won't have many other slightly infirm
      eighty-year-old men,
to help you achieve that diverse group
      you so desperately desire.
I bring unique characteristics to your student body,
      and to your sagging
      statistics too.

And surely you won't have many, if any, other students
      whose qualities as a teacher
      are praised by many, a teacher who
would be a built-in evaluator of your sometimes lazy and
      gossipy faculty, who,
I am afraid, inadvertently cheat you of money and
      sully your name
      while they
      hide behind the
      closed and locked
      door of tenure, that
glutton who never stops tearing strips
      from the shank bone
      and carcass

of your good name.

Rest assured, by the way, that I will not tolerate
    bad teaching,
it is dull and ineffective and wastes my precious time.

No, I won't stand for that.
And surely you won't have many among
    the bright-eyed youth
you normally accept, who will know the pain and fear
    of illness and disease
    that lie in wait
    from youth to age,
disorders that have already had their way with me,
like cancer and sepsis and weakness and falling that
    result from
    complications of age and
    lead to dynamic displacement
    of vital parts
    necessary for upright living.
They make a potent force to mix with unsuspecting youth.

And surely you will have few, if any, others who
    have known lifelong love,
an ever growing passion that changes form
    with passing years
    but never falters
    or flickers.

Instead it remains a vital inner force that
> spills out on life to
> make the ugly beautiful
> and the thoughtless kind,
and plows through the difficulties of life
like an ice breaker through solid arctic waters.
No, you won't have many like that.

"All right," you say, "but even so,
what would you do in your remaining years
that could justify our investment of
> money and time.
Tuition, you know, even our current
> outrageous sum,
covers only a part of your residence here.
What could possibly make it worthwhile to
> invest in you?"

Ah, this is the part you may not understand.
You will have to look beyond your
> practical noses
and imagine a Shakespearean scene,
where witches stir and cauldrons bubble,
and take a leap of faith.

You can expect *nothing* from me,
save the magic of adding to a container
> that is almost full,

unlike those of your usual bright-eyed vessels.
You have a right to expect them to take your offerings
    and do something
        with them,
though neither they nor you know what
    it will be.

In me you have a unique opportunity to add life
    to day-old soup,
to gamble on a product heretofore unknown.
It would be a reaction between long life and the future,
between mellowing of age and the excitement of
    peeking around the bend,
much as those new-car headlights do, turning without
    seeming to move,
their light shining around corners without bending
    in the prism of
    prior experience.

You must gamble that stirring new with old will
    make something useful
    in ways none of us can
    possibly foresee.

If you do it and it works, you will gain renown
    in the eyes of your peers
    and others may gain
    from the spread of the

how's and why's of
compassion and learning.

And if together we fail, no one will know the difference.
How can you turn down a gamble like that?

Even at Eighty-Two

To learn
in your last years
is to open
an ancient dusty volume
and find unexpected
coins of gold.

Piano Class[3]

May 31, 2009

Nailed to the piano bench
by lifelong desire,
I was able today
to make the music rise up
from the belly of
the Steinway whale.

I leaned deftly from side to side
to avoid the indecision
of Jonah's grim fate,
and coming cleanly
to the listening ear,
made Wilna and Felix
proud.

The Eighty-Year-Old Piano Student

I sat as
Vladimir and Artur sat,
back straight,
wrists poised,
head high.

Only I can see the
jagged blue lightening
crackling over
my knobby fingers,
making them move
as they do in
my dreams,
helping me
wring from the keys
music so beautiful
it almost satisfies
even me.

They say
it is the journey,
not the destination,
but getting to this stop
along the way

would be almost
enough.

Watching the Man in the Moon After Sixty-Two Years

We stood last night
and watched the moon,
the soft yellow complexion
of the man who lives there unchanged
from when we watched him
over sixty years ago,
a warp in time that
curves its way
past the past.

We walk haltingly
but certainly,
hand in hand for
as many moons as await us,
our hearts more full of love than ever,
always amazed
by the wonder of it all.

The Autumn of Life

We walk the path slowly, knowing
we are like the distant trees,
whose colored leaves grasp
their branches fiercely
in the chilled autumn air,
holding on to the bitter end.

The scent of the
late rose is so pungent
it brings tears to our insides,
watering the love that
still grows there.

We stop frequently to rest,
to hold one another, to kiss,
then walk on, grateful but still
looking for another
bend in the road.

A Literal Man's Thoughts on Eternity

Even the cowboy
who rides into the sunset
doesn't have it right.
The sun doesn't "set,"
the sun doesn't "rise,"
it sits immobile in the darkening sky.
There is no last sunset to ride into!

So we'd rather sit in comfortable seats,
holding each others hands,
and ride our giant Ferris wheel
through "earthrise" and "earthset,"
ad infinitum,
having made the exciting discovery,
there is no last sunset to ride into!

My Wants

My wants are few,
peanuts in shells and brown paper bags,
soups that pour thick from spoon onto tongue,
and milk, very cold milk, without too much fat,
and bread, warm crispy bread, with dents and
small holes for melting butter to hide in,
and pie, apple and cherry and rhubarb
    in season,
and oh, for a slice of Mom Manda's grape pie,
that nectar of labor and love from the past.

I also want days of sunshine and rain,
and flowers that blossom with
pistils erect and stamens all dusty,
and I want love that wraps 'round my heart,
with memories of passion and
lust of the monogamous kind,
and health, good health,
since I know that word needs
adjectival color.

And I want our grandchildren close to me,
it is to them I am most closely bound.

These are my wants, in a nutshell,
as it were.

Old Age is the Cage Where the Infant Stays

It has taken all my
eighty-three years,
to understand old age, that counterpoint
to the infant stage of silken body and
eyes that shine with innocence so intense,
it shames onlookers to silence.

Innocence isn't lost,
as so many believe, but gradually
is buried under battered beams
and pounded roofs, and windows
into the soul that are locked and closed
to exclude disappointments, evasions,
and lies.

It is used instead to build a jeweled vault,
to store and protect the Essence, which we
then carefully dispense to selected others,
who pass our way not knowing
what is hidden deep inside us,
as we know not what is hidden
in them.

Yes, old age is the cage
where the infant stays,
squalling and gurgling,
and hoping we'll care enough
to look through its eyes
at the innocence still lying within.

Will I Know It When I Am Gone?

I learned long ago from the immortal Bard,
"all the world's a stage and
the men and women merely actors,"
but though his words are famous,
the Bard left out the private stages
we little men act our plays on,
each with curtain after curtain to be parted
 in turn,
our personal acts and stories.

I already have opened most of my curtains,
and now I stand downstage center, before
a curtain that appears very old.

I wonder if this is my last curtain, and I ask,
if I step through it from now to then,
will I find nothing ? Or will there be
dust of the ages on some structure or place,
to reassure me as I take my last bow,
that I will know it when I am gone?

Part Two - My Jewish Heart

I Am a Jew

I am
a Jew. My middle European genes made me
five-foot-two, squat, bald, rounded. I look
a lot like those millions who were stripped
of hair, and teeth, and possessions, and
incinerated. I do not smell
of the ovens but I carry the ashes
of every victim on my shoulders,
the shochets and the peddlers,
the red-wigged wives and the little girls,
who played dreidels on the floors
of the shacks and hovels of the Pale, and ran
from Cossack swords that seemed
to materialize from nowhere
in the dark night.

The weight
of all who died is on me, a past that
colors my thought and behavior,
no matter the fools who deny
the terrible acts of the past.

Yet, I have great gifts
non-Jews do not have, except for those
I have given them by inheritance.

The Torah is mine,
it gives me history and pride, it shows me
human men and women striving like I do.
I march proudly beside them,
trying to understand and apply the rules,
exploring conundrums,
soaring with the poetry,
reading the stories told on the parchment
by the storytellers
of the ages.

Like those Jews, I am puzzled
just by being here,
puzzled by the continuous venom
of anti-Semitism.
There are so few of us to have been
the brunt of poisonous thought and action
through the centuries.
Even now the miracle of Israel
is a burr under the saddle of many, instead of
what it should be, a joy to be praised,
that a people hammered down
almost to the flatness of a tin roof
have risen to build their own place, where,
left alone, they would not hurt anyone.

As for me, I am more akin
to the small storekeeper or baker

than to the warrior kings or
payes-wearing fundamentalists,
the little people who gave me
the genes and the drive to rise
above the everyday to be
doctor, counselor, father, and then
Zayda to my five young people
entering the maelstrom of life as a Jew, whether
they like it or want it or acknowledge it.

Yes, I am a Jew.
I am filled with love of life,
grateful for family,
grateful for Torah,
needing at least another eighty years to understand
and apply the principles of the ages
in any meaningful way.

Why haven't I said
anything about God
in all this bragging, you ask?
God, that's a whole
other story.

An Old Jewish Man Remembers Christmas[4]

Spruce needle smell and crackling logs,
wind in my face on a snowy night,
a thick, wooden sled rumbling ice-rutted roads,
a Lionel train and bronze William Tell,
shooting pennies unerringly.

A small Catholic church,
with pews curved smooth,
where I made believe it was okay
for a young Jewish boy to kneel
as long as his knee cleared the bar.

Even as a child
I absorbed the message.
Peace and good will to all,
and I sang *Silent Night*,
that saintly refrain,
that makes you look upward, to someone
who thought he had figured it out for Jews
called Hebrews,
only a short time after that first Christmas night.

And though I understood little,
I instinctively knew there must be a place
where this message was one,
no matter what cloak of faith you wore, perhaps
in the heaven Catholic celebrants claim,
perhaps in the end of days
Jews pray for.

This nativity scene plays out in my mind
at this time every year,
in the memory of friendship and love, and
the story of a bright starlit night,
when this incarnation of good,
first was told.

KADDISH

Ancestors stutter through my heart,
like an old nickelodeon,
kept alive by the Kaddish,
given to me to say proudly, until it is
my turn to hear my children speak
these words of ancient praise
that tie the dead to the living,
and celebrate the lives
that came before us.

We grow old before we learn
that eternity is neither time nor place, rather
it resides in living memory,
in the history of a people
who survived rejections and expulsions,
reviving like small pine nuts that crack
in infernos of carelessness
to grow again, a people who, even in the
frozen barracks and pits of human ash,
knew that memory and praise were required,
that despite all the living hells
(or perhaps because of them,)
they could make our forebears live on
in the recitation of the Kaddish,
while they gave birth to a generation

that would inherit the requirement to remember,
and whose own children
would one day speak the sacred words
to inscribe them in the pages of
living memory.

Late Erev Shabbat

The flames gutter,
smoke curls and rises,
the seventh day has begun,
the gift from God which extends
the kindness of Shabbat
to man and animals
alike.

I smell the hot wax
and say the Sh'ma,
my daily homage to the author
of this time of quiet.

Erev Rosh Hashonah
5769/2008

I sit in the crotch of the giant oak tree,
over the synagogue our fathers gave us, and I watch
dozens of tiny figures in black hats and payes,
rise as smoke from the chimney spout.

They dance in ecstatic pairs
until they melt into the words
of the Talmud and Torah,
and ascend Jacob's Ladder
to be blessed by who or whatever
God is.

Then they return,
for me to decipher and read,
just as they have for 3,000 years,
so I'll know all there is to know,
about living the rest of my life.

My Grandson the Red Bearded Cantor

His voice sounded
the shofar of tradition
as he stood before us, tallit shining
in the holy light,
kippah signifying respect
for the spirit of awe
that rose from the music
of the shechinah,
and came to rest on the
ancient scrolls.

Eyes sparkling,
we leaned forward to touch the notes
with our tallitot as they sang by, the soft strum
of the guitar a youthful sound
behind the Hebrew songs, an aching call
to heal the world,
until the prayers ended
and we sat in a legacy of silence
and love.

From Zayda, With Love

The Bible says that
God closed the Garden of Eden,
and evicted its gardeners
into a cold world,
with only brief clothing
to keep them warm.

But there is a new midrash
that tells another story,
the seeding of tiny Gardens of Eden
all over the world.
I know about them, because
I work in one.

I have a big advantage over Adam and Eve.
I already know the creatures
God so laboriously gave them,
birds and fish and four-legged animals
that cavort and play around me.

But
my work involves more complex creatures
than Adam's and Eve's,
the human equivalent, perhaps,
of miraculous manna, which fell

unannounced from the heavens above when
Moses' minions were starving.

My "crop" is my grandchildren,
and I am the Zayda who tends them.
My work is guided by the many years
I have spent getting old and fat and bald,
just the right ingredients for
trust and thoughtful silence,
for love and patience
and an ability to listen, a tool
that often is more important than speech.

Oh, it is true,
my garden has serpents,
much like the Eden of old,
some live inside my crop.
Anger and fear and even self-hate
gnaw at their insides unseen, and outside
under the tree of knowledge,
envy and greed await,
feelings that lead to our holding on tightly
to what we should give away freely.

But this is where I come in,
my job is to spray each of my plants
with generosity and knowledge,
tzedakah and compassion,

in time for them to take root.

But we Zaydas must hurry.
By the time we live long enough
to be minimally wise,
our crops are almost mature and
our window of time to
weed and nurture and feed and harvest
is small and vanishing before our eyes.

So we move rapidly
to cultivate and fertilize our valuable crop,
so it can grow into the next generation of Zaydas
for the next generation of
tiny Gardens of Eden.

But then, that's what
Zaydas do, isn't it?

Part 3 – Shades

Night Stories[5]

I saw the west
through the eyes of lonely old men
dying in hard iron beds painted white, lined up
on a hospital porch of old yellow brick, built
when they still were young and strong,
still riding hard-muscled, sleek-sided horses
behind long-horned cattle
and unbroken mustangs.

These were not figures in the movies, they were
the last of the real men they modeled,
hard-bitten on the outside and soft on the inside,
alone in their last days, turning away
    from their cancers
    and heart failures
    to memories of
    the miles they rode,
from Monument Valley to Santa Fe,
from the high plains of Texas to Abilene
and Dodge, wide-brimmed hats and shiny oil slickers
    flapping in the breeze,
trail dust deep in the creases of their faces
and the crow's-feet around their eyes, the
    saddle leather
    creaking with each easy roll

of their strong, young hips
and long, leather chaps.

They were men hardly more than boys, bringing
    honor and strength
    and a strong sense
    of righteousness
to their days of sun and sweat and
    rain and snow and wind
    that made them
    pull their hats down
    over innocent, clear eyes
    that took in the scenes of this life
    that lasted only the
few years they rode, until they were old
    before their time,
and now to their quiet confusion, to sickness
they couldn't understand.

They lay in the dark and talked to me, their
fatigue resting on unaccustomed pillows,
their faces shining once again with their bygone
time of strength and courage, and
a wonderful foolhardiness, that led to
    all-out galloping races and
    Saturday night dances,
    to target shoots and
    horseshoe ringers,

to short-sheeted bunkhouse beds and
    the clang of the iron triangle
    that called them to
    hot baked bread and
    fresh-churned butter,
to beans that doubled as breakfast and lunch,
to fresh made stew of venison or elk, and
to apples that crackled with the crisp of
    each first autumn bite,
the shine of the bright red skin brought out by
    the cold mountain nights.

They remembered bedding down on
    frost-covered grass
before a rising campfire, in front of caves
scooped from shale and stone,
and marked with tracks of field mice and coyote,
    the sounds
    of cattle milling
    in the moonlit night,
where even the youngest of them could
    count the stars
and follow them home, where each trail was
    new and fresh,
and beckoned them on with never a thought
    that one day they would be
    broken and saddle sore,
telling their memories to a man so young,

they knew he was a doctor only from his
    old-fashioned, high-collared,
        side-buttoned doctor clothes.

But they talked freely. They knew
I would walk with them on that last trail,
past the sagebrush into the creek bed that led
    down the mountain
to the dark desert night, where a grave waited
in a pauper's field that likely would be marked
    with nothing more
    than a plain wooden cross,
showing only that a God-fearing man
    had passed this way
and stopped here to rest from his short ride
    into the west
    and back again,
until he and all the others laid down to die, still
talking stories of the west they lived,
not quite alone in the night, for as they talked,
they reached out to the solitary listener, sitting
on the top rail of their last corral.

Sixties Flashback

Janis Joplin's voice did it, brought back
    the long night watch of
    a generation of pain and sorrow
    during that set of years
    when our world was ruled by
    hollow men who confused growling
    with courage.

They sent half the young to grow up
in steamy jungles and ankle-deep paddies, their
camouflage almost a joke to the tiny, patient men
    who already had fought
    their own kind for centuries,
then for twenty years the French, whom
they ground into the mud,
day after day,
year after year,
until they just gave up and left, without
even worrying they might not look manly.

We could have been hiding
behind the treaty room's curtains. With
hardly a missed beat we concocted a new war,
from an imaginary shot across the bow
    in the Tonkin Gulf,

a dangerous waterslide for our soldiers
    who were expected to
        mop up the Geeks,
(they called them names, you see,
it was easier to kill them when they had
    repulsive names,)
it was easier to believe these tiny men
    could be squashed,
they wore no uniforms,
their feet were bare, hell,
they couldn't even speak English.

Well, everyone knows this part of the story,
half a generation dumped into the heat
    and swamps
    and ambushes
    and body bags of
    Southeast Asia,
then rejected, vilified, and cursed when those
    who made it through
    got home.
Fifty-eight thousand of them never made it at all.

What happened to the ones who
    escaped the draft
    or just plain didn't
    give a damn is
    just as sad.

They went to school but held class in the street,
they took courses but cursed the professors.
Oh yes, I know, I was one of the professors
who found it hard to handle
three or four hundred long-haired men and women,
no baths, no bras,
and the foulest mouths God ever permitted,
young people so disillusioned with parents
    and leaders and armies and wars
    and buddies who went off smiling
    and came home addicted
    to Vietnamese-purchased,
    Pakistan-grown,
    poppy-based heroin,
only to find the half at home high on weed, and
shooting up just like they did in Nam,
smoothing out the bumps in the road with
    reds and yellows and booze.
It turned out the half who stayed at home
    was doing the same things
    as the half who went away,
but with no mud, no blood, no waving flags.

They got high enough to live through
    Kent State and Madison,
to take over offices of deans and professors,
to confront all the other straight folks who either
    couldn't figure it out or

    who bent a little
    and grew long hair and
    spoke the jive.
I never could grow my hair long, the jive
    was easy.

What did they do besides skip classes
    and march in the streets
    and shoot up and screw?
Yes, this was when the pill was invented that
freed cute young things for sex without babies,
though surely not without the risk of
    syphilis, gonorrhea,
    chlamydia, yeast infections,
    and herpes,
but no one worried about these things yet.

What did they do?

It's hard to say whether they followed
or invented the icons who spoke to them
    through rock and roll,
Elvis and Mick and Keith and Lyle, and
    most of all, Janis,
who showed them how to screech obscene and
fall down drunk, and scream words of rebellion
    and hatred and love
    and longing and insecurity

and fear,
and sometimes even singing clearly enough
   to be understood.

And don't forget sadness.
Janis personified for all the rest the terrible
   sadness amidst
   frenetic movements
   of feigned joy,
the sadness of tears that hid behind their hearts
   and splashed unnoticed
   down their cheeks,
an incongruity of major magnitude for people
   who appeared to be
   having so much fun.

Not many generations have such
 a central figure, a symbol of all that was wrong
   with the world,
a plain-faced, death mask of a woman, angry
   beams shining from eyes
   drenched in sadness,
moving back and forth on the stage with
   jittered movements
   as though she was running
   from the demons within her, and
perhaps she was.

And the screech—part night owl and part hawk,
    part ghost and
    part vulture—a
sound that mouthed itself around the
    fear and emptiness
    of the disaffected young.
She held it up for all to see and gain strength
from the joint sharing of its sadness, its emptiness,
its glaring upward in shock at imminent
    drowning in a sea of
    straitjacket ties
    that lay waiting
    for all those who
    would be carried away.

Yes, Janis led without knowing, flaming
in and out of life as clearly as jets flamed
    from the sky
    in faraway Nam.

It wasn't too many years before it was over,
hair cut, drugs covert,
music countable and soft,
the names of the dead carved in black granite
    outside the
Washington Monument, people sighing
as they deflated to other wars, other generations.

There always seem to be plenty of kids
    ready to suit up
    and fight and die,
while the old rockers march off
into the darkness with few to follow them.
That part, at least, seems different.

There is no end.
The sixties are over but
the camouflage lives on.

It's the Boogie![6]

Oh, let the boogie roll
out down and dirty,
let me feel it in my bones
and up my spine,
let the keys tease me
with "can you
roll the barrel with
Ammons and Johnson,
Mary Lou and all the others
who rode the boogie to the last
of the low keys
and played the highest
of the right hand half steps?"

How I wish
I had felt free enough to
roam the back-alley clubs
and smelly dives
where the heavy hitters
split the night
with a beat that shook the bricks
and rattled the shots of whiskey
they used to oil their joints with juice
that hid the ratholes where the
boogie rested between sets.

It was a hard, gut-strung sound
that jammed people from the
four count to the eight-to-the-bar.
It lived in the walls of their nights
and lifted those who beat their feet
and twisted their bellies
to this hard-assed music,
'til they arrived at a bright new place
in an otherwise dirty and
often rhythmless
world.

The Biplane Bicycle[7]

I climb on my black,
repainted $5 bike and
take the stick of the
WWI Sopwith Camel
I fly every Saturday matinee
against The Red Baron.
My mechanic shouts contact,
the engine sputters and roars,
he pulls the blocks,
and with my silk scarf flying,
I take off from the
grass-covered runway
and head east across
the channel,
free of childhood
with its petty fights and calls of
"fatty, fatty run for your life."

Those days are hidden
under blankets of time,
my black bike is gone,
the sidewalks now are
softened by sunshine.

But when I ride my new red bike,
the wind still blows through my hair
and I pedal with the panache of
goggles, a white silk scarf, and
a classic leather jacket
unzipped halfway to make room for
the thrust of my prideful
chest.

Night Driving[8]

The road was shiny under
a close-up moon,
the center line an arrow
pointing the way,
only a rare, splattered bug
spotting the eye.

We drove the night in a poverty
that never was real to us,
rich in love and prospect,
needing little,
wanting little,
knowing that things are not
the substance of riches.

We rode on
dad's Standard Oil card,
peanut butter and jelly,
baloney and mustard,
small withdrawals
from the bank of reality,
warding off sleep with the
mountain wind blowing
through the open window,
the shadows of primeval hills

stark against the moonlit sky,
the stars rounding every turn
as though tied to our bumper
like tin cans at a wedding.

We arrived tired and sleepy,
rubbing a scratchy beard and
burning eyes,
with both our gas tank
and stomachs empty.

5917a Theodosia[9]

MAY 10, 2008

5917a Theodosia is gone.
Black children run empty lots
where a red brick house stood, the street
agape, raw gums,
teeth yanked without novocaine, rotted boards
hiding paint-peeled window frames,
door frames, store frames,
defiant weeds flanking dead gray steps
to porches abandoned to wind that whistles
across sagging planks.
An occasional drunk lurches
down cracked sidewalks where
a blank-eyed woman sits, hopeless, dreary.
It is the end of the earth, and some
have already fallen off.

Part 4 - Those I Love

Marion's Visit to the Amish

September 13, 2008

I saw joy today—pure, ebullient joy, it welled up
from the storehouse of youthful memories
    that still resides
    within her.
The sight of this plain people made
    her step quick
    and her eyes bright,
as she negotiated each rain-covered walk and
    stepped into our Utah past.
The white houses peeling paint stood in sharp contrast
    to manicured lawns
    and bright flowers,
red barns and old-tyme pies,
warm bread, cookies, cakes,
weavings and rugs, a saddlery and woodworks,
and black-box carriages whose reins were held
    by bonnet-headed women
    and small girls, whose
shy smiles and bare feet were no more
out of place than men's bearded chins
    under clean upper lips
    and black hats.
Their outhouses differed from the past

  only in the tin drain
  plainly marked "Men,"
their draft horses and carriage ponies and
   colts and mares and
   fields of corn and hay
   and clover cut
   through by dirt roads
acknowledged the present only where
   they had to touch
   county asphalt.
She almost skipped into the happiness
  of a remembered past,
shared more than they knew with this people
  who live outside time,
and who gave her her best day, today,
without their even trying.

After a Visit

I am lost in
broken heartstrings
when a loved one goes home.

I use them
as little boys use string,
to tie two tin cans together,
then I hold my can
tightly to my good ear,
and wait impatiently
for news of their return.

The Well of Loneliness[10]

Death and I have stood
time and time again
at the edge of the well of loneliness, he smiling
quietly, knowing he will see every soul
beckoned by the dark waters, I weighed down
by sadness.

It is the loss of the young ones that is hardest,
but their loss has taught us that only by grasping
the hands of those who gave us life
can we remove the barb that twists in our hearts.

It is family that connects
from past to future, connects
us to those who will stand by us
when it is our turn to enter
that well's watery surface. They
are proof of our place in line.

Their names are:

ESTHER SCHWARTZ,
my mother's mother.
She stood long hours in a tiny store,
dark shelves of tobacco,
candy, thread, conveniences
of immigrant life, only one small,
high window bringing sunlight
to poverty's dusk, shining on
a round, wrinkled face, braided
long hair wound in a bun, in a
shapeless print dress, rooted in
the old country, reaching out to
the new. She had me read to her
for years, but printed English
was beyond her, but not love,
not strength, not wisdom.
Ninety-six, or so we guessed,
when she slipped away in
uncontrolled bits, she lived a
little too long.

SIMON SCHWARTZ,
my mother's father.
Burly baker from Bialystock,
handsome shock of brown hair
framing a smiling, crinkled face,

bushy brown moustache,
dressed in his best and only
brown suit, vest, tie, fedora to
visit me weekly. He stood at
the bottom of the stairs shouting
my name, climbed to bring
me toys, games, love, died
at home in his bed at age forty-four, of
Hodgkin's disease, surrounded
by family, friends, surrounded
in my memory by a blinding white
light beyond the capacity of
any electric bulb then extant.

ANN SCHWARTZ PERKOFF,
my mother. Gave me square feet,
identical wrinkles, a burning
desire to read, learn, live, gave
me awareness of music, dance,
and art so intense it hurts, taught
commitment to family, work,
love, fought for her children
by living their lives, adopting
their ways. She stood so firmly
in one son's shoes that it
destroyed her brain when he
died. She dangled her feet
over the dark well for years

before she disappeared
beneath its surface at age
eighty-three.

Rose Perkoff,
My father's mother. Petite,
grey hair pulled back in a
bun, glasses, soft speech,
kept a cow in the back yard
in her earlier years, made
strudel dough so thin yet
so strong you could hold
it up and see light through it
without a break. Raised five
children almost alone, my
Dad was number four. She died
in her eighties.

Chaikel (Ike) Perkoff,
Dad's father. First in the family
to travel the long, tortuous path
from Moscow, was a tinsmith
but he couldn't get work
in that trade, ran a filling station
instead. He sat straight and
proud at the head of the Seder
table that filled their small
living room on Minerva Avenue

across from my grade school.
He dressed in deep crimson robes,
a brilliant tallit, and tall crimson
inverted-stovepipe kippah
through interminable Seder
prayers. But I remember them.
I learned their lessons, carried
on through my childhood by my
Dad, and then into my own family.
Ike died in a filling station explosion
when he was in his thirties.

Nat Perkoff,
my Dad. Wonderful, scrappy,
tough man, small in size, big in life.
We bonded when I was a boy,
grew closer later in life, partners
in keeping Mom functional. From
boyhood on we walked and talked,
he telling me the things I needed
to know man to boy, me telling him
what he needed to know to
understand my life, boy to man.
He took care of Mom, a woman
who lived on the hard edge
and sometimes was hard to love,
but had a spunk and creative
brilliance that attracted him and

all who met her. Died at eighty-four of
heart failure and pneumonia.

STUART Z. PERKOFF,
my brother. Shorter even than me,
smarter than me, combative,
rebellious, funny, black
hair thick over full eyebrows,
eyes steely-black. Drugs,
anarchy, women, the Beat life
dragged him down but poetry
lived in him from age thirteen on.
Poet was his occupation,
consigning him to the low end
of common life, even as he
soared to the heights of beauty and
fell to the depths of ugliness.
Died at forty-three of lung cancer.
As he lay dying, he pointed
a bony finger at me and said
"I trust you!" It was the best
gift he possibly could have
given me.

Lottie Maizner,
Marion's mother. I know her name
was Charlotte Evelyn but I always
knew her as Lottie,

the second mother God gave me.
She is almost as much a part of
me as my own mother. The name
"Lottie" represents home, safety,
love, dependability, fine cooking,
wisdom, making the most of little.
She gave all her goodness to
Marion, whose family and mine are
forever entwined. Lottie died of
thyroid cancer at sixty-seven.

Isidore Maizner,
Marion's father.
Tall, handsome,
hale-fellow-well-met.
Always ready with handshake,
a story, fine bourbon,
the best table in the house.
Behind his warm smile was
the reality of a daily grind on back roads
to small towns and merchants,
selling work clothes
not everyone wanted,
constantly reaching for the brass ring
and missing, but never letting on.
Even a stroke didn't stop him,
though he had to slow down,
had to have someone else drive him.

He hated it. Died of another stroke
at sixty-three.

Roslyn Maizner Singer,
Marion's oldest sister.
Bright, rebellious, independent
but too early for feminism,
feared missing out on life,
stayed home for Wash U,
but should have flown away.
She married late, had two children,
both now gone, Alice, at age twenty-nine,
Jim, after Ros had died, at fifty-three.
She nearly drowned in the dark waters
after Alice died, but recovered,
spent years in therapy and helping others.
We would talk of art and travel and books
and life and her eyes would shine and
her speech would elevate to new
heights of animation, but she missed out
on the practical side of life,
much as a high-wire man misses a step
and falls to the net, but for her
there wasn't always a net.
Ros died at seventy-seven.

HENRIETTA MAIZNER HOCHSCHILD,
Marion's other sister.
Beautiful, original, creative,
saw the theme in each project,
each party, each life.
Knew how to boost others' lives,
another feminist before the feminists' time,
a free spirit with flair.
She too lost an adult child, Steven,
and never was the same again.
Yet she emerged from angst and depression
to be excitingly outlandish,
adorned her body with
unique clothing, jewelry, hats, coats,
adorned conversation with wit and laughter.
But despite all her efforts,
remained aware of the ever beckoning
well of dark waters in which
she lost her loved one,
wasn't sorry to join him.
Died of liver failure at eighty-two.

ALICE SINGER,
Roslyn's daughter
in more ways than one.
Independent, inventive,
knew what she wanted and
set about getting it,

loved Greek anthropology,
made folk dancing her academic life.
Hired by UC Berkeley, she
was killed by a turning truck
while on her bike
preparing for her new life
that never came to be.
She was twenty-nine.

STEVEN HOCHSCHILD,
except for Stuart,
the closest to me of these young
lost from our lives.
He radiated ideas, creativity,
there was action with every word,
every plan, every new approach to the world.
Caught up early in the young people's
rebellion at Columbia,
he turned his zeal into action,
developing among the first
university distant learning systems.
Married Chris, our families
and the world are better places for
his having been there. Died at thirty-seven.

JAMES SINGER,
Ros's other child.
GREW up in Alice's shadow,

broke out of his shell
on the high mountains of Tibet,
became a dealer in Thankas and Gneshas,
traveled the world widely,
bringing back stories and art to sell,
but was fooled too often
by fakes and fakirs.
He fell into debt, saw
the well of loneliness,
liked what he saw, and
to our horror, jumped in.

Yes, Death and I have stood together
too many times at that awful well
and know loneliness at its darkest
in the loss of the four gone
much too soon—Stuart, Alice, Steven, and Jim.
Knowing how to swim will never
keep us out of the dark waters,
but looking back and climbing up
the strong rope of family
tells an eternal story of continuity
for those who follow,
so they will know at least as much
as we about those who already
have entered the deep water of
the well of loneliness.

A Promise Kept[11]

I drive the
early morning streets,
sun-dappled trees
rushing past the anxiety of my somber task.
Crying leaves fill me with sadness as
I walk through the silent woods to Babler creek,
the water waiting.

I open the small grey box and
throw ashes into the fast cold water. Only then
do I find chips of bone in my fingers,
and really know, for the first time,
what I am doing.

I turn
with the empty box and stumble back, tears
in my eyes, my heart pounding,
my breath caught on the thorns of sadness, overwhelmed,
my promise kept, but I,
usurper of this Godly task, am
devastated.

Mom at Sixty-Eight

She was sixty-eight,
 kicking and screaming on the floor,
her anger flooding the tangles and breaks
in an infantile tantrum
she still hid behind closed doors.

Then came an almost postictal quiet,
broken only by sobbing and sucking air,
until the junctions spliced again
and she could emerge as she was before,
working the crowd with a head toss
and triumphant smile.

But she could not win against time.
 Her eyes slowly glazed
as she slipped through
one crack after another,
finally crawling back into
diapers and crib.

Then the mumbles.
Then the spittle.
Then, nothing.
She was eighty-four.

The Color of Love

I awoke peering deep
in her beautiful brown eyes, colored now
with fear and the loyalty of love.

How many times has she
looked into my soul
as it was slipping slowly away,
shining the light of her eyes
into the land of shades
for me to climb back once more
to my place by her side.

We rose together from
the path of darkness, and holding
cuffs as high as aging steps permit,
resumed our journey
down our own tumbling brook, over
the pebbles and pathways
assigned us.

Part 5 - Looking Around Me

The Apple Tree

Icy winds swirl
through branches
bent as an old crone's cane,
their hard sap sealing cracks
to hold life steady until
soft white blossoms promise
crunchy red fruit and
kitchens steamy with
fragrant cobblers and
crisp-crusted pies
cooling.

Voyeur

The morning sun lights
the skeletons of leaves
in bas relief
like women's shapely legs
seen through slipless skirts,
sexy, provocative, and
desirable to every man
who peeks.

6:30 AM

This is my
witching hour,
opalescent dawn,
the checkerboard of
fresh mown grass,
the low hum
of the earth
toweling off
its morning bath.

EVENTIDE

It is
eventide, the earth turns toward me
with her shoulders covered in gold and lace,
and leans slightly forward to welcome
the sun to that secret place
where he prepares for
tomorrow.

The Autumn Solstice

God's thumb
gently tilts the Earth away from the sun, maples
choose from palettes of colors,
and paint themselves red overnight, just as
Indians painted their faces to show courage
for what lay ahead.

How small
are the changes that herald the seasons.
Slight shifts in the sky bring cool air, where
yesterday gentle warmth stood, and
colors to signal the snuggling of leaves
under the blanket of winter, until
His thumb tilts the Earth back
to springtime and summer.
Meanwhile, we sit in our balcony seats
and lean back and watch in wonder.

Cold Autumn Tree

Only straggler leaves remain,
dull colored remnants
turning in the wind
in their need to hold on.
Then, one by one, losing,
futile, falling, dark.

Will their mother miss them,
she of dark, thick trunk and
dry, varicose bark,
as she awaits new
seasonal sap?

No, she has no awareness,
heart, or consciousness,
gets no love from
her compost children,
feels no parental pain,
just stands and waits
for winter's end.

Black Hummingbird[12]

Oh, nugget of coal
with gift of flight,
why are your feathers
black as night?

Cousin to bright colored kin,
are you a trick,
played on aging sight?

Or are you proof
in darkest flight,
that Darwin, all along,
was right?

Summer Morning

Summer morning air greets me
with its promise hiding behind
a hint of sweet tasting moistness,
its wall of quiet moving back
every now and then to let the sounds
of early-bird workers pass by.

As I watch,
the sun rinses gray from the eastern sky,
its warmth speeds up morning's birdsong,
and my wakening heart beats in rhythm
with the new day.

Summer Night

The black summer night
is my friend. It fills me with the smell of
grass, tree, and leaf, its darkness
swirls on cool breezes that caress my face,
my arms, even my toes,
with the touch of a lover who lies in waiting,
his ardor fueled by the same night breeze
that draws me near.

As I sit there,
the blackness lightens, stars and
incandescent lights gently brush back
the deep soot blanket,
until I can almost see.

Then I sit,
suspended between dark and light,
wake and sleep, excitement and
a rare bliss that tells me what it means
to be alive.

Part 6 - Meditations

Locker Room

We all are naked under our clothes,
bellies sagging, scars
and striae making a map of the past,
crevices open to scratching, much as
the baboon and chimp sit in satisfaction
in the crotch of a tree and
saw away at their itch.

I can see them now, leaning back
with that superior smile,
chewing on a leaf or straw,
scratching and grunting without,
as far as we know, a care
in the world.

We are
closer to them than we think, in
some ways even less civilized,
in our consummate self-interest,
our unthinking use of force, even
our ability to reason may get us in
more difficulty than they ever knew.

But we alone can dress, and become
whoever we want to be.

The Shadow of Your Smile[13]

Turn, my love,
that I may glimpse
the shadow of your smile,
a translucent shade
that brushes my heart
with memories
yet to be tendered.

Smile, my love,
that I may glimpse
this hologram of your soul,
here for the instant that times it,
then gone with a turn of your head,
leaving beauty and
silence behind.

Sounds

Can you hear your mind?

Sometimes mine makes
the high-pitched whine
of a circular saw,
cutting each board
to the quick.

Sometimes it speaks
with the full-throated cough
of a fat-bellied Harley
that leaves me helplessly
behind.

Or it might be whispering with
the almost audible breath
of Elizabeth's black, shiny Rolls,
idling in the wet British night.

Sometimes they all shout together,
raucous, disorganized furies.

And then there are those fleeting moments
when voice after voice is silenced, until
only a crooner sings.

The Potter

I dream
I am a potter
with a spinning wheel,
and fingers of steel
that shape formless clay
into graceful pots
that smell of earthy woods,
each one with a tiny crack
in the mud-caulked prison
where the spirit of beauty
lies.

I release her
with a lover's kiss,
and she rises from the mud
to love me back.

Then, taking my
clay-clogged hands to her lips,
she smiles and disappears,
leaving me to search
the wet leaf-sharp-smelling woods
in vain.

Then I stop and say to myself,
"I am a potter,"
and with my fingers of steel,
I shape formless clay
into a mud-caulked prison,
and I lie down inside to
wait for her.

What Would Peace Look Like?

What would
peace look like?

Would it be
the smooth, curved sound
of a seashell held
to the ear of
a child?

Or would it be
the horizon moving
as the earth sighs
in relief?

We hang on
the straps of
a carousel world,
and imagine
through gaps
in the darkness,
that we'll be
here to see it
when it comes.

Visiting Old Notebooks

As I thumb
through my old notebooks,
the still unselected poems flirt for my attention
with fluttering eyelashes, exotic
perfumes, and sometimes a carefully
dropped strap.

We are a family of sorts.
They sprang from my soul when it sang truly, so
I liked them enough to save them.

I read them
as they lie in their bed of lined pages, and
once more fall in love with the words, the images,
the occasional rhyme.

I pick some, and
try to explain to the rest why they
must stay behind.

For Jim[14]

His spirit
walked the room above the crowd, greeting
each mourner with the same gentle openness
he always showed—listening, smiling,
placing each one first, for him the "other"
always came first.

It didn't seem strange,
this contact with his spirit.
If anyone could turn and wave goodbye
before going on, it was him,
always thoughtful,
always ready with a kind word, a helping hand.
It had always been this way,
why not now?

He listened
to his granddaughter sing the love
that made this day just another stop on a road
now turned around the bend.

Friends extolled his virtues, family
bared their hearts to show their love, their respect,
while from his place above us
he spoke of the future,

assuring us he will always be with us
in the steps of our daily rounds,
in the wrinkled brows of our problems,
in our collegial contacts, day to day,
week to week, month to month,
still setting goals and daring us to reach them,
and promising to reserve a place
for us at his side.

Raindrops on the Eaton Sculpture

There must be millions of raindrops
    hurtling downward
    from row upon row
    of high diving boards,
pausing first to screw up their courage,
then falling, hair flying, arms out,
eyes wide with the finality of it.

The lucky ones collect for just a moment
    on the florid colors of
    this whimsical outdoor
    sculpture,
    hang there,
and then look below,
pick out a landing place,
and gently slide down
the remaining air.

Lady, Are You There?[15]

I don't know
if they really saw you, but
you were there for them.
You followed them to the beach
on those moonlit nights when
the surf sounded your words, and the seagulls
turned one eye from their nightly dreams of soaring
to the dome of the bright blue sky,
and moved to make room for
Stuart and Tony and Frankie, who
sought you in the drug-driven night.

They shot up, sang
to the moon, saw visions of you standing
tall in the sky or sitting on their shoulders,
and they wrote, in books like this one,
what you gave them.
We can read it today and see the inner fiber
that tied horrors to loves, beauty to pain, and
marked out their private
pathways to hell.

I had no idea
words would come to me,
but they do, in the day or the night,

when I am silent, or making the noise called language
that tells others the inner man I am.

Sometimes
the words make torrential rain on the page,
but sometimes they come slowly, painfully,
plucked from my brain as one
would pull a buried splinter
from its berth deep in sensitive flesh,
but come they still do.

Do you give them to me now?
I turn my titanium-locked neck from side to side,
trying to see you on my shoulder where Frankie says
you sit now, but I can't see you or feel your weight or
the beat of your heart.

Yet where did the words
come from if you are not there?
They started in the little bookstore back room,
when someone pulled the bung from the barrel
full of my thoughts and feelings and
sometimes painful memories that turn up
at the end of my pen and leave their marks on the pages, so I
can read them and know what they say.

Could it be that you, Lady,
someone I turned up my nose at

for all of those years, someone
I never believed in, someone who made me think
Stuart and Tony and Frankie were just crazy enough
to see you from their perch on the end of a needle,
could it be that you really do
sit on my shoulder now?

Part 7 - Coming of Age

Fatty, Fatty, Run for Your Life!

"Fatty, fatty, run for your life, here comes skinny
    with a butcher knife!"

The words cut through the hot air radiating
    from the dark red brick
    gangway walls,
the two houses leaning inward, crushing me,
compressing the heat into my nostrils
    and panting mouth
    as I ran from the shrill voice,
footsteps pounding the crude concrete, pocked
and spotted with the brown impurities
    of cheapness.

No, he never caught me.
Even a fat Jewish boy can run fast when pursued
by a skinny goishe kid with a knife,
even though both of us knew the knife was just a
    figment of fear and oppression
    that hung over my head
    like that guy Damocles,
who lay tied tight under a suspended sword,
a gleaming instrument that seemed made,
not of steel but of the sharpest glass, another

fear to be thrown on the rough pile of all
    the others I had accumulated
    by the time I was six or eight,
living with ignorance.

Yet, I was ignorant too, what did I know of
Catholics, Methodists, Presbyterians?
I was smart but I couldn't even spell much less
understand all the words that classified the kids
    who lived on that
    tree-lined street
    called Theodosia.

Those were the depression years,
but it was a better place to live than many. Our
house was a two-story flat,
built of deep, dark red brick,
with five concrete steps we used to play
stepball, throwing the ball hard against the
flat surface, but trying to sneak a hit on
the pointy edge.
If you were lucky, the ball would fly right back
to you, and you could make a one-handed catch,
just like I saw Joe Medwick do.

I used to see him close-up when I went to
    the Cardinals games,
at Sportsman's Park at Grand and Dodier, take

the Easton Avenue streetcar to Grand Avenue,
transfer and ride the Grand Avenue north through
the negro neighborhood (we didn't use
the words "black" or "African-American" then,
we were much more likely to use the "N" word,)
    get off at Dodier and
    cross Grand,
head for the back gate to far left field, find
the sign for the "Knothole Club,"
and sit on splintery bleacher seats. I always
tried to sit where I could see Joe and he
    could see me,
so if I was real lucky he might throw me
    the last out
    for a souvenir.
He never did, but I always took my glove,
just in case.

But it did happen every time I played stepball.
Then I played left field alongside Joe. Never
in my wildest dreams did I ever replace him.
We played side-by-side along with
    Dizzy and Paul
    and Pepper Martin.
Oh, how unhappy I was when Diz got hit
    in the leg
    by a line drive,
and insisted on continuing to throw, never

  got over it,
never recovered completely,
then was traded to the Cubs, of all things. Can
you imagine, the Cubs?!

But the steps weren't only for stepball.
They led to a concrete walk, then
four more concrete steps by three dusty
basement windows framed in black,
the eyes of a monster staring.

No, you never rubbed off the dust, never
looked into the black basement.
You walked straight ahead until you came
to an ornate, green-black door, with
carved panels and a brass doorknob,
all out of place in this simple and otherwise
unadorned neighborhood we now would call
"blue collar" or "lower middle class."
But we knew it as just "mixed" enough
to keep you on your guard.

The heavy door opened silently to a stairway
  of dark wooden steps,
each with its ridged-rubber pad nailed
  carefully from left to right
  and front to back, yet
still always coming loose.

The inside stairway was steep—
fourteen or fifteen steps at least.
I used to stand at the top and watch Zayda Schwartz come for
    his weekly visit.

If you went straight after you got to the top, you got
    to the bathroom—
odd placement for a utilitarian space normally hidden in
the recesses of a house—perhaps we were less modest,
or more practical than we thought.

A U-turn from the entry led past a long railing
into my tiny bedroom at the front of the flat, two
bunk beds, I had the lower one.
My brother Stuart must have gotten the upper one,
though I have no memory of his ever having
been in that room.

A left turn at the top of the U led to
the living room, with torshears groaning
under the weight of thick panes of leaden glass,
so dark they seemed to hide rather than
transmit light. Two large windows
looked out on the street, where
they too became the scary eyes of a
block-headed monster in the dusk of even fall.

The living room opened into the
    master bedroom,
with the kitchen at the back of the house with a plain
metal sink against the inside wall.
I was discovered there once or twice standing
on a chair, peeing during a midnight sleepwalk.

The back door opened onto a stairway to
the back yard, no grass, its primary attraction
a catalpa tree that grew lady fingers a foot long
that make foul but mischievous cigars to smoke
    when they dried out.
There was a rickety, half-collapsed, one-car garage
    beside a large
    cement ash pit,
and a narrow walkway led to the alley, which was
transformed into Sportsman's Park whenever
the Manda boys and I played stick-ball or
cork-ball, the name dependent upon
whether or not we had a real ball
    or an improvised one
    out of cloth and string.

The bases were spread down the alley for about
    the length of two houses.
The bright sunlight and dusty, rough alley bricks
    made an eerie fill for the spaces

    between the sagging, narrow garage doors
        that guarded their dank and dark interiors—
empty until the dads came home and somehow
        maneuvered their one and only car
        into its waiting slot.

A boy is lucky to have real friends. Mine were
Vic and Joe, the Manda twins, the youngest in
the family of our ice man, Daddy Manda, whose
arrival with his horse-drawn wagon we awaited
    with bated breath
    on hot summer days.
Sitting on the concrete steps, seeing the horses
first, and then the wagon turning the corner
    as though in a dream-like mist,
    dripping water from melting ice
    hidden under drenched tarp,
running to meet the rig and waiting anxiously
for chips of ice, given with silent smile
and an amused shake of the head,
pre-air conditioning cooling that expressed
a loving and common sense approach to small boys,
then following Daddy up the steep stairs to
    the ice-box that had
    one compartment for food
    and another for
    a fifty-pound block of ice.

And becoming part of his family through
    the alley games
    and ice chips,
learning later that I had met the Mandas
    much earlier.
Elsie, the twin's older sister, had been my
    first baby-sitter,
and Dad and the oldest Manda boy, Leo,
    had been tennis partners
for years.

Together, we were exemplars of a tolerance
    we didn't even think about,
a Catholic and a Jewish family for whom religion really was
    what so many people
    say they want it to be,
nothing more and nothing less than
a set of principles to live by.
There was no room for sniping remarks or vicious fighting,
no room for derogatory rankings,
a vision most don't follow through,
any more than amateur golfers swing the swing
    they see in their minds,
    but never can execute
    with their hands.

Mom was the center of my childhood,
though Dad and I were close,

we had different life viewpoints.
His efforts to teach me to box to fight off bullies
were foiled repeatedly by my unwillingness
    to hit anybody,
the start of lifelong avoidance of conflict
    that became a
        major life characteristic.

I was enchanted by weekly trips to the art museum
and the zoo with Mom, though their number
may have been inflated in my memory
because of my love for them.

We'd climb the wide marble steps to
bright golden doors that led to a sculpture hall
    as big as another world,
the light slanting in from back windows on
valiant Greek warriors and muscular Valkyries.

The impressionist and abstract works stand out
    from the other galleries
        of paintings. Even then
I was drawn to what we call modern art.

And I can still feel my fear of the dead Egyptians,
    tightly wrapped bodies
        of dead Pharaohs,
reminding me always of the hard-hearted Pharaoh

who made us tremble
every Passover Seder.

Mom's love of books and constant reading led
to my incessant reading that continues
    to this day, and she always
insisted that I "go look it up" when
    I couldn't spell
    or understand a word.
I always asked "How can I look it up when
I don't know how to spell it?"
She never let it pass, "go look it up," was
    her constant refrain.

Perhaps this would have turned
    someone else off,
but the effect on me was just the opposite.

Books became my friends, my support,
for didn't she demand the same commitment
from herself, reading in an almost
gluttonous way, like she had discovered a new food
and was gorging herself on it?

She would read everything there was to read,
about Nijinsky,
about Diagelev,
about Ted Shawn,

about Martha Graham.
Not too many other little boys were brought up
on a diet of art and dance and books and libraries
and museums and galleries and painting
    and sculpture.

She was what today we would call a liberal,
openly having friends who were homosexual,
today's "gay" people,
though their lives are anything but "gay" in
    the old sense
    of that word
    that we have lost completely
    in our "other" gender and
    transsexual world.

Dad was the practical teacher,
but I failed at boxing,
even failed at bike riding at first, falling off
a tilting two wheeler repeatedly
until balance finally came,
so I could ride my bike
    far from home.

We did run together long before
the jogging era.
We'd set out from the house, left on Theodosia,
then left on Hamilton, running

all the way to Natural Bridge Road,
where the Small Arms Plant was during the war.
Dad would work there later,
after we had left the neighborhood
    and I was in college
    and medical school.

He would run easily, I would
run out of breath quickly,
then huff and puff until I could rest
    at the end of the line.
Then we'd repeat the same path in reverse.
I don't remember ever being able to do it
    without getting winded,
but I gritted my teeth and did it.

Mom did more than enjoy books and art,
she worked tirelessly with blind children and adults.
Sometimes one of the boys from the
Missouri School for the Blind spent weekends
with us.

Troy was his name, he was slight,
with blonde curls and vacant blue eyes.
I learned early about people who had it
    much harder than I did,
who could not see, sometimes could not hear,
    sometimes both.

Helen Keller was Mom's heroine.

Then there were the adults like George Kraft,
who lost his sight to broken glass
and his left arm to its unfortunate placement
    outside his car's window
    in an accident that took away his life
    almost as effectively
    as if he had actually died.

I can still see him tuck the box of matches
in the armpit of his missing arm
    and strike the match
    to light the cigarette
    that dangled unseen
    from his lips.

And there was another, now nameless, slim man,
    who always was sad and
    wore a neatly pressed topcoat
    and old-fashioned hat.
Mom took him food and Braille books and
conversation and company.

Mom's assignments always were coordinated by
    Miss Ruenzi of the
    School for the Blind,
who was herself blind, but a great fighter

for the rights
of the blind
and the deaf.
We were proud to know her as "Miss Ru."

The depression years surrounded all we did,
there was no money.
Dad once had to sell Realsilk hosiery on the road
    in Texas,
and once got a telegrapher's job
on a New York paper.

We pulled up stakes and moved for that one, but
the job evaporated as soon as we
got to New York.
I don't know what paper it was,
only bad memories fill that time,
Mom hiding her sunburned misery
    beneath a bath towel,
the only thing she could stand to wear,
feeling lost at Jones Beach, the sand
spreading out for miles,
no memory of playing in the surf or swimming,
or even talking with anyone,
no memory of Coney Island,
though family talk said we went there often.

But those months stay vivid because of

just one moment,
coming home from school to a
    harsh, spittled voice
    that rode the banister
    down a long dark stairway.

A woman wrapped in a nondescript robe
stood at the top, staring hatred down
    the staircase,
a single lightbulb burning behind
    unkempt red hair,
harridan is the only word for her.
"Get out of here, you damned Jew," she said,
"I kicked them out,
your father couldn't pay the rent!"

I turned and ran, uncounted lampposts went by,
cars, people, I was lost, drowning, finally
I got hungry and wandered
the aisles of a dime store,
looking from side to side, seeing no one,
past a bin full of large chunks
    of milk chocolate,
stole a hunk, shoved it into my shirt,
walked out the door,
lost myself in the passing crowd,
began to gnaw at the chocolate,
and then heard "Jerry! Jerry!" and

saw Dad driving by looking
    for me.
If I had turned in the other direction
he wouldn't have seen me.

We moved to the lower east side,
where the dingy, brown tenement that
sits dimly in the back of my memory
    seemed barely able
    to stand upright
    after four generations
    of immigrants
    had passed through.
The pale yellow light shone in windows of the night,
the streets below were dark
in the canyon of top floor vision.

I have no memory of these tenements in the daytime,
only darkness and kitchen smells and
a circle of boys who must have been Jewish,
because wasn't everybody there Jewish?

Our major accomplishment was to steal some
potatoes and build a fire on one of the roofs
    to roast the potatoes
    in the ashes.
We burned our fingers pulling them out, ate
the half-raw potatoes while looking over

the parapet at the dizzying heights
    and then got sick
    and vomited it all up.

For years I couldn't go to New York without
    physical discomfort,
even when I was there on business almost
monthly. Only when we came to New York
    for plays and musicals
    and museums
did I finally grow out of this childhood phobia.

When we returned to St. Louis
my childhood expanded. The Mandas
had bought a farm outside St. Louis near
    tiny Union, MO,
small white house under old oak tree,
tiny yard on a dirt country road, woods
    on the other side,
dusty red barn with stalls for horses and cows,
hayloft opening on the barnyard through
    wide wooden doors,
chickens wandering the manure-matted yard,
    pecking and picking
    and clucking away
    their numbered days.

Draft horses with sassy, wide hips pulled the wagon

and the plow.
I rode behind them on the high wooden seat,
their haunches rotating as opposite half circles
    of durability and strength.
They seemed impossibly larger than
Daddy Manda as he wrestled the single-bladed plow
behind one of the enormous horses,
turning the black dirt over the last remnants
    of wheat or oats or grass,
      following the path of the previous row
      'til the field was black with straight lines
    and smelled of moist, rich loam.

Vic and Joe and I roamed the woods,
soft sunlight illuminating the oak and maple leaves.
They taught me about moss on trees
    and garter snakes,
and when I "had to go" they would build me
a "throne" of two stacks of flat stones
    where I could sit
    in comfort,
using young tree leaves instead of the
Sears Roebuck catalogue that graced the outhouse
    back at the farm.

Vic and Joe pulled me into adolescence
    as much as I was pushed
    by my early testosterone,

they were five years older than I was and
    they could drive.
We would go to town dances held under moonlight
    on wooden platforms
    that shook with the heavy-footed
    dancing, flirting, loving
    that went on.

I can remember seeing beer bottles but
    never seeing drunks,
don't ever remember dancing myself, certainly
did nothing sexual, but it was heady stuff
    for a twelve-year-old who
    looked older than his actual years.

I loved it, never saw any harm from it, still
remember those hot summer nights,
    riding to and from town
    in the '35 Ford two-door.

Joe usually drove, while I listened to the V-8 engine
hum on the night road,
the yellow dashboard light shining on the curved,
    single-arc shift
    vibrating quietly
    between the front seats.
If I ever got into classic cars,
the '35 Ford two-door would be one of the first

I would look for.

The little farmhouse had enough of
    a dining room
    to hold a round table
    that sat at least eight.
We had dinner there with lots of pork chops
    and mashed potatoes
    and vegetables from the garden.
Even though we didn't keep kosher in our reformed
Jewish household, we didn't push the envelope
too far out in those early days.
I never saw any harm in pork chops.

The real treat at the Mandas was Mom Manda's
grape pie—crisp crust, pie filling bubbling with
    concord grapes, all
    peeled and seeded
    before going in the mixture.
My mouth waters to this day at the thought of it.
I even got it for breakfast.

Years later, Emma Manda appeared at our
front door one evening when we were having
    a big dinner party
    holding a grape pie
    as a special gift for me.
She was the only one besides Mom Manda

who ever made it.

After grade-school graduation, we moved from
    Wellston, a mixture of
    Jew, Catholic, and Protestant,
to a suburb called Normandy, no doubt named
    after that section of Catholic France
    that years later took the lives of
    thousands of American boys
    scaling the beaches and cement piles
    that made them ducks in a barrel
    for the Nazi gunners who
    waited above them in
    dugout, underground
    bastions of death.

Little did I know that I would become a target
    in a different way,
    a short, bright Jewish boy
    who set out for
    Normandy Junior High School
    without knowing anything was amiss.
After all, hadn't I lived among all kinds of
    different people
    without running into
    the vicious meanness of
    childhood anti-Semitism?

My previous life of Catholic acceptance
    and Protestant disinterest
lulled me into a dreamlike state of
    blissful ignorance.

Only a few of these bad memories remain.
Danny, a slim, freckled Irish kid towering over
my short Jewish body and taunting,
    "Where are your horns?"

Strange kids whose names I didn't even know,
walking across the street on Lucas and Hunt Road,
    throwing rocks and
    calling names,
their hatred mixed with grudging admiration
    for my stellar
    classroom performance.

I went out for football to show them all
    what I was made of,
making the football team as a 175 pound
    twelve-year-old.
I was the slowest, fattest, shortest second-string
    guard in history.
 In my first practice scrimmage,
knowing nothing, I was ground into
    the dust and dirt,
    feeling bewilderment

    more than pain,
then I felt the cleats and saw the
muscular leg and gritted teeth and murderous
look on the face of the star quarterback,
    Pookie Aussicker,
his heavy foot coming down on my left knee.

This single event had more effect on my life than
any stardom in high school football
    ever could have had,
including surgery to remove
the medial meniscus from my left knee before
I went to medical school so I would be able
to spend the hours on my feet required of
    medical students
    and doctors.

I only played in one real football game,
    an "away" game
    late in the progress
    of the back and forth
    unskilled shoving that
    determines the outcome.
We must have been way ahead or the coach
    never would have
    put me in.

My main recollection of this stellar event is

  lying on my back
  looking up through
  the dust at the lights
  glaring down on the field
  and into my eyes,
feeling even at that game-sharp moment
  the oddity of my
  even being present
  in that unnamed
  small Missouri town.
I understood even better than before
  the incongruity
  of my football career.

The other time I was on the playing field was
  the only game
  Dad had ever
  come to watch.
He saw me running out onto the field and
  believed he was
  going to see me play,
but in a foretelling of my future life, I had been
  sent out to help
  bring off an
  injured player.

Normandy High School didn't spend much
money on uniforms and protective clothing

in those days, and injuries
like my knee and
whatever was wrong
with that poor and
now long forgotten
unnamed boy were very common.

I tried to make it in other fields of athletics,
to show those tough Germans I could do
    whatever they could do.
I was the sixth man on a six-man tennis team
    for which only six
    had tried out.
I put the shot and threw the discus on the
    track team,
    but in my usual
    second-string slot
    never participated
    in a meet,
a sensible decision by the coach, for I could not
    throw either of these
    inanimate objects
    very far.

I did do everything else that was required of a
    track team member,
down to and including running a mile after
    every practice.

I was so slow that after I lumbered my way
    over the packed cinders
    for a mile and came
    back into the locker room,
everyone else had gone home and I was alone
with whatever the suppressed psychological
    motivations were
    that made me do
    such a silly thing.
I never thought of it then, but there never was
    anyone there to see if
    I had actually done
    my mile.

I could have gone home early.

I also was the goalie on the soccer team,
primarily, I always believed,
because I filled more of the space across the
    front of the netting
    than anyone else.
I can still feel the heavy blow of the
    mud-covered ball
    in my belly when
    I stopped a score.

I did play in some of those games and still try
    a little soccer kick when

I come across any
unattended ball
and no one is looking.

Fortunately, there was another sport at
which I did excel, and that was learning!
I made excellent grades, even in the
mathematical byways that were my weakest
    stops on the way to
        valedictorian status.

But my major place to shine was under
the tutelage of another person who was
out of the mainstream of the school culture.

Ernestine Long was her name. A stocky,
red-faced, gray-haired woman,
wearing a short, white coat and skirt of the same
    laboratory cloth,
stained with chemicals and dust of many years
    of contact with the desks
    and benches of the
    chemistry laboratory
    of which she was
    the queen,
        though the word "queen" is probably incorrect.
If I had been more sophisticated than young
teenagers were in my early years, I would have

realized that, almost certainly, she was my
    first recognizable
    lesbian.

I knew a little about difference from
    being Jewish, and
    from my mother,
and, instinctively, I loved Miss Long,
who was the first to stand in my corner
    and wipe my brow
    and apply styptic pencil
    to the cuts and bruises
    on my intellect.

She taught me the academic religion
    called research
    that became
    and remains
    the mantra of
    intellectual success.

The darkness of the laboratory and
the solitary nature of the work did not
inhibit our minds or dampen our enthusiasm
    for the problem,
which was the then current uncertainty about
    the sites of
    digestion and

absorption of vitamins, particularly vitamin B1.

I realized that we could mount a glass retort
    in a rocker
to mimic the burps and gurgles of the
    human stomach,
add varying amounts of acid and, after "digesting"
the vitamin in the flask for different lengths
    of time,
we could test for its presence and learn if it had
    been digested,
    and "where."

To our great excitement, and contrary
    to current belief,
the vitamin B1 remained unchanged
    over a wide range
    of concentrations of acid
    and shaking times in
    our primitive motor mount.

I don't suppose anyone today remembers
    "Believe It Or Not" by Ripley,
but this cartoon-like feature was in almost
    every newspaper
    in the country with oddities
    that no one would "believe,"
    and I was one of them!

"Fourteen-Year-Old Boy Builds
Artificial Stomach,
Studies Vitamin B1 Digestion!"

We still have the time-yellowed paper
    in a scrapbook
    downstairs in
    our storage room.

Ernestine helped me feel grown up outside the lab too,
letting me drive her one-seater '35 Plymouth coupe
    to pick up something
    we needed for an experiment
without really questioning my statement that I knew
    how to drive a car. But
    there I was,
tooling along busy Lucas and Hunt Road
as though I knew what I was doing,
picking up our needed item,
and then returning without incident.
It was a good thing I was able to pull straight
into her parking place,
I would have been in trouble if
I had had to parallel park.

I never heard from Ernestine Long
after I left high school, and for many reasons

I never went back there,
so I don't know if she shed what must have
    been a difficult
    and lonely life,
but I also have never forgotten her.

I didn't do as well on my next drive,
to the Club Plantation, a dark jazz joint
    at Delmar and Grand
    where I took piano lessons
    from Cozy Cole,
a large black man whose hands
could reach twelve keys.
He was another of the many natural players
I met in a life of seeking the key to piano stardom
    that always turned on me
    and demanded talent and
    hard work in addition
    to desire.

When Edith Coggins and I
went to the Plantation after our junior-senior prom,
I backed into the car parked behind me.
It was a small dent and I drove off frightened,
    hoping the driver
    wouldn't be too mad.

My latter high school years were good,

with a friendly rivalry with Bob Lovell for
    valedictorian of our class—
an honor we ended up sharing.
His later life was much less happy than mine.
He didn't get to go to college and succumbed
to the boredom that dooms some
    whose lives fall short
    of their dreams—
he took his life years later.
Sadly, I heard of it long after the fact and
    could only go on doing
    what he would have
    wanted to do but
    couldn't.

But in our senior year we both prospered,
sharing books, debates, the valedictorian stage.
I don't know if he made it to the senior prom,
but he would have enjoyed the trick Edith
    played on me.

I had asked the class blonde beauty
    Edith Coggins
    to the prom,
and she amazed me by accepting!

We danced cheek to cheek, she

in her lovely formal, I in my summer tux
   with white coat
   and black pants
   and glistening shoes.
We went to the Club Plantation afterward,
much as F. Scott Fitzgerald's heroes and heroines
   went slumming
   in their formal dress
   and shiny shoes.
When I took her home, I asked if
I could walk her to the door and kiss her
   goodnight.
She said "No, my husband is standing right
   up there and he
   wouldn't like it."

Back then, girls who married in high school and
   were "found out"
   were expelled.
She had wanted to go to the prom,
   so she went with me.
I didn't really care, I had a great time and have
   had this "trick"
   memory ever since.

Though I shaved at an early age, during these years
   I was a downy-cheeked
   a boy looking for adulthood,

and I found it one day when the car radio spewed
    the blood and fire
    of Pearl Harbor.

I was driving up Lucas and Hunt Road, heard
the events that would lead to five years
    of millions dying,
and ran into the tavern at the entrance to
Velda Village to confirm the terrible news.

Velda Village, a quiet collection of
    brick bungalows hiding
    behind a brick arch,
until then a peaceful place where I walked
    to and from school,
    after that, a place
    of dark memory.

I grew older that day, sobered by
    the specter of death
suspended in the air behind me like
    a black balloon
    in the Macy's
    Thanksgiving Day Parade.
He plucked my friend Louie Soffer
off the beaches at Normandy a couple
    of years later,
leaving a hole in my heart and Louie's

Schaeffer pen
in my pocket.

Yes, I know you haven't met Louie,
he was part of my college life.

College was the expected path for me as long
    as I could remember.
Neither Mom nor Dad had gone beyond
    Central High School.

We turned down a scholarship to Harvard
    without thinking about it
    one way or the other
    for lack of train fare
    and dormitory fees.
Can't imagine that happening in today's world,
    where college acceptances
    hang from one's belt
    like scalps on
    Indian breech cloths
    in the old west.

Washington University was fine for me,
I didn't even consider it a second choice.
I took a service car from Lucas and Hunt Road
    into the Wellston Loop
    only a few blocks

from Theodosia,
where we used to live,
then the City Limits streetcar to the stop in front
of Washington University.
Long, narrow, divided tree-lined street through
large grassy acres to
a wide, stone stairway to
turreted castles on the hill,
administrative buildings for the university that
once were the main buildings
for the 1904 World's Fair,
now the gateway to a quadrangle that
looked just like the quads in the movies.

How many can put a finger on the moment
their unconscious search
becomes purpose, ambition,
desire?

I had two such times,
the first buried in childhood with a mother who,
like many other Yiddish mothers,
wanted me to be a doctor,
(didn't all Yiddish mothers want their
sons to be doctors?)

She devoted hours, days, years, to shaping
an immature intellect,

not by discipline or pressure but by exposing it
    to art and books and
    music and dance,
showing by example the wonders
    the mind makes
    and what it means to
    help all those others
    whose lot in life
    left them at the bottom of
    the ladder or hole or jail
    in which they found themselves
but could not climb out of without a helping hand.

I was not led by bridle and muzzle, but instead
    was set on fire with love of all
    those things of the mind that
    came from her heart and lodged
    tightly in mine.
There never was any question in our minds
    about my goals and
    how to attain them.
How fortunate I was that she still was around
    to share them.

The second moment I found at Ridgely Hall at
    Washington University.
My friend Eddie Satz introduced me to a girl
    who stood there smiling,

pin curls showing under her patterned scarf,
the belt of her camel's hair coat tied loosely
    in the current style,
grey plaid slacks, brown brogues with split tongues,
her sparkling eyes lighting the hallway outside
Mr. Arnold's freshman English class.
It was February, 1943.

We fell in love and later were married, but that is
    another story for another time.

Notes

1. In 1955 I survived a malignant melanoma of the neck with positive nodes.
2. Memories of a near death experience.
3. A small recital just for adult students.
4. Childhood memories of Christmas holidays spent with my Catholic friends, the Mandas.
5. Stories told to me during my night patient rounds when I was an interne.
6. Dedicated to my brother Simon, a great boogie player.
7. My first bicycle.
8. Each year we drove to Carmel, CA to the annual meeting of the Western Society for Clinical Research, driving at night to avoid the desert heat.
9. After we had visited all our childhood homes.
10. Written in memory of those who left us much too soon.
11. Marion's sister Ros asked me to spread her daughter Alice's ashes after she died, in St. Louis's Babler State Park. It was one of Ros's favorite places.

12. Written after seeing a black hummingbird at Caneel Bay, 2/14/09, St. John, USVI.
13. Written after hearing the Tony Bennett recording of "The Shadow of Your Smile," music by Johnny Mandel, lyrics by Paul Frances Webster, 1965.
14. James C. Olson, 1917–2005
15. Dedicated to the muse of Beat Poets Stuart Z. Perkoff, Tony Scibella, and Frank Rios.